Nashville Predators

Claryssa Lozano

AV² provides enriched content that supplements and complements this book. Weigl's AV² books strive to create inspired learning and engage young minds in a total learning experience.

Your AV² Media Enhanced books come alive with...

Audio
Listen to sections of the book read aloud.

Key Words
Study vocabulary, and complete a matching word activity.

Video
Watch informative video clips.

Quizzes
Test your knowledge.

Go to **www.av2books.com**, and enter this book's unique code.

BOOK CODE

N 4 9 8 8 4 7

Embedded Weblinks
Gain additional information for research.

Slide Show
View images and captions, and prepare a presentation.

AV² by Weigl brings you media enhanced books that support active learning.

Try This!
Complete activities and hands-on experiments.

... and much, much more!

Published by AV² by Weigl
350 5th Avenue, 59th Floor
New York, NY 10118
Websites: www.av2books.com   www.weigl.com

Library of Congress Control Number: 2014951923

ISBN 978-1-4896-3155-8 (hardcover)
ISBN 978-1-4896-3156-5 (single-user eBook)
ISBN 978-1-4896-3157-2 (multi-user eBook)

Printed in the United States of America in Brainerd, Minnesota
1 2 3 4 5 6 7 8 9 0 19 18 17 16 15

032015
WEP050315

Senior Editor Heather Kissock
Art Director Terry Paulhus

Photo Credits
Every reasonable effort has been made to trace ownership and to obtain permission to reprint copyright material. The publishers would be pleased to have any errors or omissions brought to their attention so that they may be corrected in subsequent printings.

Weigl acknowledges Getty Images and iStock as its primary image suppliers for this title.

Nashville Predators

CONTENTS

Introduction

The Nashville Predators made their home debut on October 10, 1998, in Nashville, Tennessee—also known as the Music City because it is the home of country music. In a league with 30 teams, the Preds become the 27th NHL organization to take the ice. Like most young teams, the Predators struggled as they developed, posting losing seasons in each of their first five years. In year six, they finally reached the postseason before being eliminated by the Detroit Red Wings.

After three years in Dallas and four more in Pittsburgh, James Neal was traded to Nashville in advance of the 2014–2015 season.

Immediately following their first **playoff** berth, the Predators returned to the postseason in three straight seasons. Each time, they were unable to make it beyond their first opponent. Their playoff victory drought continued until the 2010–2011 season. That year, the team defeated the Anaheim Ducks in the first round. The Preds also won another playoff series the following postseason against the Red Wings. They continue to take aim at winning their first Stanley Cup in **franchise** history.

Up-and-coming center Colin Wilson played in 81 games during the 2013–2014 season.

Nashville
PREDATORS

Arena Bridgestone Arena

Division Central

Head Coach Peter Laviolette

Location Nashville, Tennessee

NHL Stanley Cup Titles None

Nickname Preds

1
Coach of the Year Award, won by Barry Trotz

7
NHL Playoff appearances

51
Most Wins in a Season

19
Playoff Wins

History

5 different players have captained the Predators during their first 15 seasons.

David Legwand was the first player signed by the Predators. He played 15 seasons in Nashville— more than any other Predator in team history.

For years, Richard Evans, the chief executive officer (CEO) of Gaylord Entertainment Company, tried to find a professional hockey team to play in Nashville. In 1995, there was talk about the New Jersey Devils moving to the Music City. However, those plans fell through. It was not until 1997 that businessman Craig Leipold was approved to purchase an NHL franchise. Nashville was to be the home for this **expansion** team. Over the next few months, the president, manager, coach, assistant coach, and executive vice president positions were filled in Nashville.

In September 1997, Leipold and the president of the franchise unveiled the team's **logo**. In honor of the 10,000-year-old saber-toothed tiger fang and foreleg bone, which were found in Nashville 26 years prior, the face of the extinct animal became the team's logo. Ever since, all apparel worn by the players and their fans had the same fierce face and distinct look. Finally, a contest was held to name the team that would bring hockey to Nashville. In November 1997, the team's name was revealed, and the Nashville Predators were born.

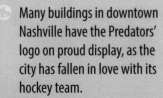
Many buildings in downtown Nashville have the Predators' logo on proud display, as the city has fallen in love with its hockey team.

The Arena

The old scoreboard at Bridgestone Arena required enough energy to fuel 18 homes. The new state-of-the-art scoreboard requires only half the power.

Anew $160 million arena was built right in the heart of Nashville. In 1996, the doors opened to the Bridgestone Arena, which was known as the Nashville Arena at the time, introducing the city to a new kind of entertainment—professional ice hockey. It was on that day that the Nashville Predators played their first game against the Florida Panthers. The Preds have called the arena home ever since.

The facility was originally named the Nashville Arena, then the Gaylord Entertainment Center, then the Summit Center, and finally, the Bridgestone Arena. A stunning new addition to the arena recently took place when a new, high-definition scoreboard was added overhead. The arena has been nominated several times for different venue-of-the-year awards. With a large seating capacity, Bridgestone Arena hosts many exciting events, including concerts, circus acts, and award shows.

After fans requested more snack choices at the Bridgestone Arena, Predators' Executive Chef Wade Gnann responded. He created the popular "bacon-on-a-stick," which includes a 5-ounce (142-gram) slice of thick-cut bacon.

Where They Play

British Columbia **7**

Alberta **4**

3

CANADA

Saskatchewan

Manitoba **14**

Ontario

Washington

Montana

North Dakota

Minnesota **11**

Wisconsin

Oregon

Idaho

South Dakota

8

UNITED

Wyoming

Iowa

6

Nevada

Utah

Colorado **9**

Nebraska

STATES

Illinois

13

Missouri

California

Kansas

5

Arizona **2**

New Mexico

Oklahoma

Arkansas

1

Miss

Pacific Ocean

MEXICO

Texas **10**

Louisiana

Gulf of Mexico

PACIFIC DIVISION

1 Anaheim Ducks
2 Arizona Coyotes
3 Calgary Flames
4 Edmonton Oilers

5 Los Angeles Kings
6 San Jose Sharks
7 Vancouver Canucks

CENTRAL DIVISION

8 Chicago Blackhawks
9 Colorado Avalanche
10 Dallas Stars
11 Minnesota Wild

★ 12 Nashville Predators
13 St. Louis Blues
14 Winnipeg Jets

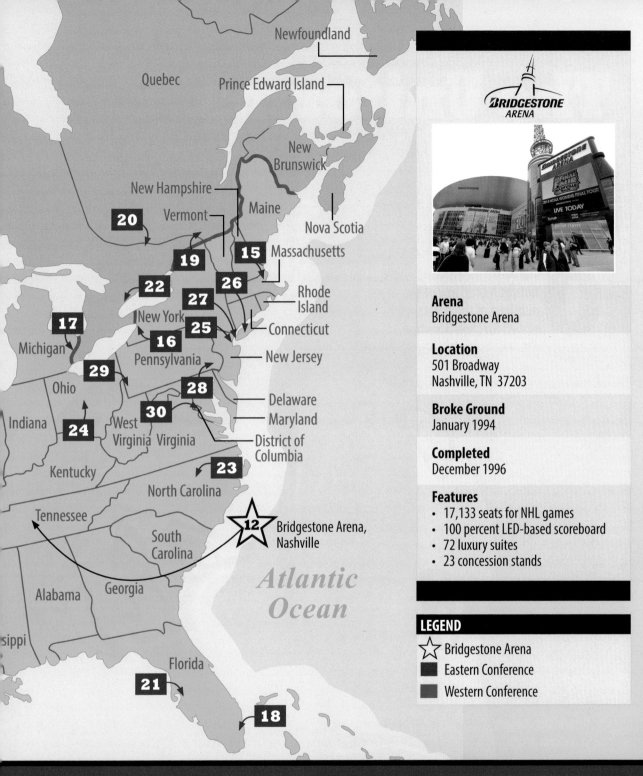

Newfoundland

Quebec

Prince Edward Island

New Brunswick

New Hampshire

Maine

Vermont

20

Nova Scotia

19

15 Massachusetts

22

26

Rhode Island

27

17

New York

25

Connecticut

Michigan

16

New Jersey

Pennsylvania

29

Delaware

Ohio

28

Maryland

Indiana

24

30

West Virginia   Virginia

District of Columbia

Kentucky

23

North Carolina

Tennessee

☆ **12**   Bridgestone Arena, Nashville

South Carolina

Alabama

Georgia

Atlantic Ocean

sippi

Florida

21

18

BRIDGESTONE ARENA

Arena
Bridgestone Arena

Location
501 Broadway
Nashville, TN 37203

Broke Ground
January 1994

Completed
December 1996

Features
- 17,133 seats for NHL games
- 100 percent LED-based scoreboard
- 72 luxury suites
- 23 concession stands

LEGEND

☆ Bridgestone Arena

■ Eastern Conference

■ Western Conference

NHL EASTERN CONFERENCE ★★★

ATLANTIC DIVISION

15 Boston Bruins
16 Buffalo Sabres
17 Detroit Red Wings
18 Florida Panthers
19 Montreal Canadiens
20 Ottawa Senators
21 Tampa Bay Lightning
22 Toronto Maple Leafs

METROPOLITAN DIVISION

23 Carolina Hurricanes
24 Columbus Blue Jackets
25 New Jersey Devils
26 New York Islanders
27 New York Rangers
28 Philadelphia Flyers
29 Pittsburgh Penguins
30 Washington Capitals

The Uniforms

0 The Nashville Predators have not yet retired any of the jersey numbers of the greats who played for their franchise.

Despite the changes in uniform design, navy blue, white, and gold have always represented the Predators.

Since the Predators joined the NHL in 1998, their uniforms have changed six times, with some shifts in their look being more dramatic than others. Their original uniforms included the team's colors of navy blue, white, and gold. Those uniforms, and the ones worn today, feature the team's saber-toothed tiger logo.

HOME

AWAY

Three major shifts in Predators uniforms took place in team history. In 2001, a mustard-colored jersey was added. Next, in 2007, Reebok Edge tweaked the team's home and away jerseys, making them a bit more sleek and modern. Finally, in 2011, a bright gold jersey was added as an alternative. The Predators' home jerseys now have a gold stripe on the pants, and away jerseys have a gold stripe on the sleeves.

Besides their normal jerseys, the Predators wear camouflage jerseys during pre-game warm-ups to support the military, and gray jerseys to support cancer awareness.

Helmets and Face Masks

The saber-tooth tiger logo appears on **ALL** Predators helmets.

Players' numbers appear on the front of their helmets in navy blue letters for away games and in gold letters for home games.

In hockey, helmets are the most important part of a player's uniform. This is because they help protect players' heads from pucks, sticks, other players, and even the ice itself. Player helmets are meant to be more about safety than style, which is why the design has not changed much over the years. The Predators' player helmets have always been either navy blue or white, depending on whether they are playing at home or on the road, with the Predators' saber-toothed tiger logo on each side.

Goalies have much more blank space on their helmets. Many goaltenders choose to decorate their head gear with their own personal flavor. In the 2013–2014 season, current goalie Pekka Rinne wore a face mark designed by artist Dave Gunnarsson. On Rinne's helmet, a Facehugger alien— which is fashioned from the movie *Aliens*—appears alongside the team's saber-toothed tiger.

In the 2013–2014 season, goalie Carter Hutton used a saber-tooth tiger to inspire fear in his opponents, only letting up 91 goals during that season.

The Coaches

15 The Predators had played under the same coach for 15 seasons and 1,196 regular season games before the start 2014–2015 season.

Peter Laviolette has never coached a team to a losing record during a full 82-game season.

From the day the Nashville Predators joined the NHL in 1998 through the end of the 2013–2014 season, the team employed only one coach, Barry Trotz. During the reign of Trotz, the Preds made seven playoff appearances in 15 seasons in Nashville. In early 2014, however, news was released that Trotz's contract would not be renewed for the 2014–2015 season. Peter Laviolette, former head coach of the Philadelphia Flyers, was hired to lead the Preds into the future.

BARRY TROTZ A year before the team was even set to begin play in Nashville, Barry Trotz was named as the head coach of the Predators. A Canadian citizen, Trotz did not know much about Nashville. However, he took the job, and quickly grew to love the city and its team. Trotz completed his time in Nashville with 557 wins, 479 losses, and 1,196 points. He was awarded the Sporting News NHL Coach of the Year Award for his work during the 2006–2007 season. He later was nominated for the Jack Adams Award, which is awarded annually to the coach who contributes most to his team's success.

PETER LAVIOLETTE New to Nashville, Peter Laviolette's first year in his new coaching home began well, as the team won 14 of their first 20 games to open the 2014–2015 regular season. Laviolette is well-traveled and a hockey lifer, having spent two years with the New York Islanders, five seasons with the Carolina Hurricanes, and another five seasons with the Philadelphia Flyers. It was with the Hurricanes, in 2006, that Laviolette led his team to a Stanley Cup title. In his 12-year coaching career, he has a total of 408 wins, 290 losses, and 906 points.

Fans and the Internet

Nashville Predators fans show up ready to cheer on their hockey team. During the 2012–2013 season alone, Bridgestone Arena was filled to capacity in 29 of 41 Preds home games.

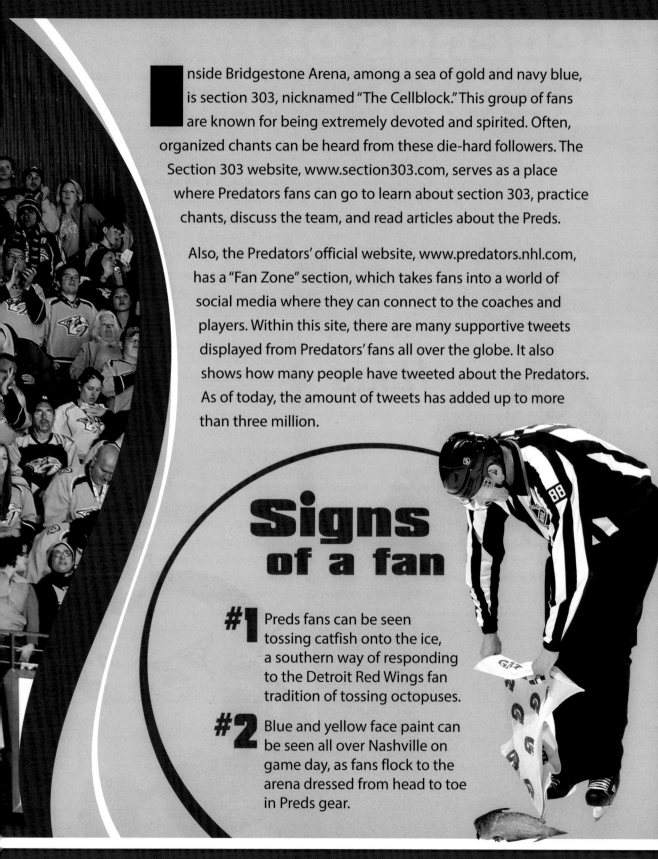

nside Bridgestone Arena, among a sea of gold and navy blue, is section 303, nicknamed "The Cellblock." This group of fans are known for being extremely devoted and spirited. Often, organized chants can be heard from these die-hard followers. The Section 303 website, www.section303.com, serves as a place where Predators fans can go to learn about section 303, practice chants, discuss the team, and read articles about the Preds.

Also, the Predators' official website, www.predators.nhl.com, has a "Fan Zone" section, which takes fans into a world of social media where they can connect to the coaches and players. Within this site, there are many supportive tweets displayed from Predators' fans all over the globe. It also shows how many people have tweeted about the Predators. As of today, the amount of tweets has added up to more than three million.

Signs
of a fan

#1 Preds fans can be seen tossing catfish onto the ice, a southern way of responding to the Detroit Red Wings fan tradition of tossing octopuses.

#2 Blue and yellow face paint can be seen all over Nashville on game day, as fans flock to the arena dressed from head to toe in Preds gear.

Legends of the Past

Many great players have suited up for the Predators. A few of them have become icons of the team and the city it represents.

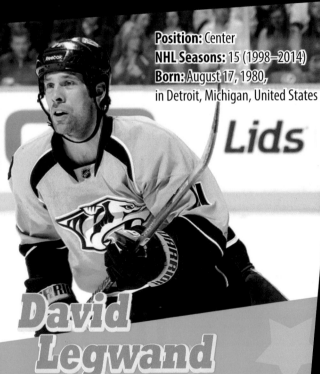

Position: Center
NHL Seasons: 15 (1998–2014)
Born: August 17, 1980, in Detroit, Michigan, United States

David Legwand

At only 17 years old, center David Legwand was the second overrall pick in the 1998 NHL **Entry Draft**. Already having won several awards in junior hockey, he showed much promise. In 2002, he was one of the first Predators to play in an NHL Young Stars Game. While there, he scored three points in one period, an NHL record. With a total of 956 games played, 210 goals, 356 assists, and 566 points, he leads the franchise in each of the four categories. He played for the Preds until 2014, when he was traded to the Red Wings.

Martin Erat

Martin Erat began playing for the Nashville Predators during the 2000–2001 NHL season. By the end of his first season, Erat had set three Predator **rookie** records for most games played, 80, most **assists**, 24, and most points, 33. He spent the rest of his time on the team carving out more scoring records while also being a model of durability and consistency. Erat is ranked second for most goals, assists, points, and games played in franchise history.

Position: Right Wing
NHL Seasons: 12 (2001–2014)
Born: August 29, 1981, in Trebic, Vysocina Region, Czech Republic

Kimmo Timonen

Kimmo Timonen played for the Preds for eight seasons. In 2000, 2004, and 2007, Timonen was chosen to play in the NHL All-Star Game on behalf of the Predators. The 2006–2007 season was his last with the team, and he went out with a bang. During his final season in Nashville, he notched the most goals and assists of his career. It was also during this time that Timonen was named captain, guiding the Predators to their first 110-point season, a record that is still unmatched in the Music City.

Position: Defenseman
NHL Seasons: 15 (1998–2014)
Born: March 18, 1975, in Kuopio, Northern Savonia, Finland

Ryan Suter

Already having won three gold medals in international junior hockey, Ryan Suter began his NHL career in Nashville. He was chosen seventh overall in the 2003 NHL Entry Draft by the Predators. In 2012, he was selected to play in the NHL **All-Star** Game alongside teammate Shea Weber. During his career with the Preds, Suter played in all 82 games during three separate seasons, proving him to be a dependable and reliable teammate.

Position: Defenseman
NHL Seasons: 9 (2005–2014)
Born: January 21, 1985, in Madison, Wisconsin, United States

Stars of Today

Today's Preds team is made up of many young, talented players who have proven that they are among the best in the league.

James Neal

James Neal is brand new to Nashville, as the Predators acquired him via a trade on June 27, 2014. The 2014–2015 season marked Neal's first in Nashville. Before this trade, Neal played with the Dallas Stars for three seasons and with the Pittsburgh Penguins for four years. During the 2011–2012 season, Neal was selected for the NHL All-Star Game. During that campaign, he scored a personal best 40 goals. Neal is known for having a quick trigger and a strong shot.

Position: Left Wing
NHL Seasons: 7 (2008–2014)
Born: September 3, 1987, in Whitby, Ontario, Canada

Shea Weber

After five years with the Predators, Shea Weber became the youngest captain in team history, directing his team to the playoffs twice. Considered elite by most hockey fans, Weber has already played in three NHL All-Star Games, and was the runner-up for the NHL **Norris Trophy** twice. In the 2013–2014 season, he collected a career high of 56 points. Weber is ranked third in franchise history for total goals and games played, all while playing a physical style of defense.

Position: Defenseman
NHL Seasons: 9 (2005–2014)
Born: August 14, 1985, in Sicamous, British Columbia, Canada

Pekka Rinne

The Nashville Predators are the only NHL team that Pekka Rinne, or "Peks," has ever played for. Although he has been with the team since 2005, he did not begin playing full seasons with the club until 2008–2009. That year, he recorded seven **shutouts** and finished fourth in the NHL **Calder Memorial Troph**y voting. In his career with the Predators, he has made the NHL All-Star team once, has been named Star of the Month three times, and has been named Star of the Week six times. He was also named NHL Rookie of the Month in February 2009.

Position: Goaltender
NHL Seasons: 8 (2005–2014)
Born: November 3, 1982, in
    Kempele, Oulu, Finland

Roman Josi

Entering the 2014–2015 season, Roman Josi, nicknamed "Yos," had only three years of NHL experience. During his rookie season, Josi tied for fourth in goals among other NHL rookie defensemen. He had been picked up by the Predators in the 2008 NHL Entry Draft after showing tremendous promise, despite his relative inexperience in youth hockey. Josi is now well-known as one of the top European defensemen in the NHL, and he continues to improve with the Preds. In the 2013–2014 season, he set personal career highs with 72 games played, 27 assists, and 13 goals, two of which were game-winners.

Position: Defenseman
NHL Seasons: 3 (2011–2014)
Born: June 1, 1990, in Bern, Switzerland

All-Time Records

16 Seconds
Fastest Goal scored in a Preds Playoff Game
Right winger Adam Hall scored a playoff goal against the Red Wings in a mere 16 seconds.

33
Most Goals by a Predator in a Single Season
In the 2008–2009 season, center Jason Arnott scored a record-breaking 33 goals.

110
Most Team Points in a Season
In the 2006–2007 season, the Predators compiled a franchise record of 110 points. It was also the only season in which they won at least 50 games.

85

Most Points by a Predator in a Single Season

With 31 goals and 54 assists, left winger Paul Kariya tallied an impressive 85 points in the 2005–2006 season, the most in franchise history. His 54 assists are also a team record.

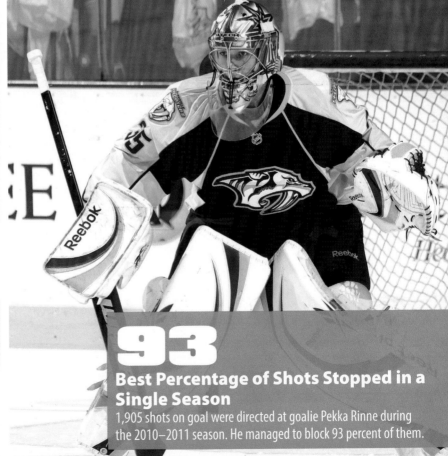

93

Best Percentage of Shots Stopped in a Single Season

1,905 shots on goal were directed at goalie Pekka Rinne during the 2010–2011 season. He managed to block 93 percent of them.

Timeline

Throughout the team's history, the Nashville Predators have had many memorable events that have become defining moments for the team and its fans.

1997
Leipold Hockey Holdings, Limited Liability Company (LLC) is awarded a franchise by the NHL, which it owns until the year 2007.

2003
The Predators' 1,000th goal is netted by left winger Scott Hartnell. The Preds win 4–3 in overtime, outlasting the Anaheim Ducks.

1994	1996	1998	2000	2002	2004

2001
The Predators collect their 100th win, defeating the Ottawa Senators.

In 2000, the first overtime penalty shot in NHL history is made by David Legwand against the New York Rangers at Madison Square Garden.

1998
The Predators play the Carolina Hurricanes and record their very first win as a franchise.

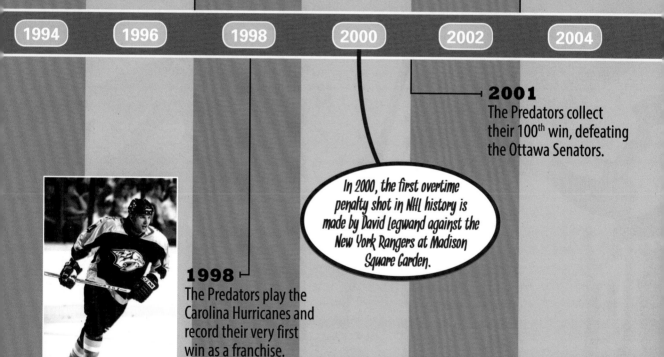

The Future

Although the Nashville Predators lost the only coach they have ever known in 2014, they have gained someone who can instruct them from a fresh point of view. Laviolette has big plans in mind for this young team, which is full of potential. It is true that the Predators have yet to reach the Stanley Cup Final, but the arrow is certainly pointed up for this young and talented franchise.

2008

Nashville qualifies for the playoffs for the fourth season in a row. In their first playoff game, the Predators defeat the St. Louis Blues, 3-2.

In 2012, defender Shea Weber signs a 14-year, $110 million contract, making him the recipient of the second-largest contract in NHL history.

| 2006 | 2008 | 2010 | 2012 | 2014 | 2016 |

2007

The Preds win their 50th game in a season for the first time in franchise history.

2014

The Predators announce Peter Laviolette as their new head coach. Barry Trotz moves on to coach the Washington Capitals.

Write a Biography

Life Story

A person's life story can be the subject of a book. This kind of book is called a biography. Biographies often describe the lives of people who have achieved great success. These people may be alive today, or they may have lived many years ago. Reading a biography can help you learn more about a great person.

Get the Facts

Use this book, and research in the library and on the Internet, to find out more about your favorite Pred. Learn as much about this player as you can. What position does he play? What are his statistics in important categories? Has he set any records? Also, be sure to write down key events in the person's life. What was his childhood like? What has he accomplished off the field? Is there anything else that makes this person special or unusual?

Use the Concept Web

A concept web is a useful research tool. Read the questions in the concept web on the following page. Answer the questions in your notebook. Your answers will help you write a biography.

Concept Web

Adulthood
- Where does this individual currently reside?
- Does he or she have a family?

Your Opinion
- What did you learn from the books you read in your research?
- Would you suggest these books to others?
- Was anything missing from these books?

Childhood
- Where and when was this person born?
- Describe his or her parents, siblings, and friends.
- Did this person grow up in unusual circumstances?

Accomplishments off the Field
- What is this person's life's work?
- Has he or she received awards or recognition for accomplishments?
- How have this person's accomplishments served others?

Write a Biography

Help and Obstacles
- Did this individual have a positive attitude?
- Did he or she receive help from others?
- Did this person have a mentor?
- Did this person face any hardships?
- If so, how were the hardships overcome?

Accomplishments on the Field
- What records does this person hold?
- What key games and plays have defined his career?
- What are his stats in categories important to his position?

Work and Preparation
- What was this person's education?
- What was his or her work experience?
- How does this person work?
- What is the process he or she uses?

Trivia Time

Take this quiz to test your knowledge of the Nashville Predators. The answers are printed upside down under each question.

1 How many Stanley Cup championships have the Predators won?

A. Zero

2 How many times have the Predators made it to the NHL playoffs?

A. Seven

3 How many coaches have worked for the team?

A. Two

4 Which player was the youngest to be named captain in franchise history?

A. Shea Weber

5 What are Nashville fans known for throwing on the ice?

A. Catfish

6 How many times has the team's current arena name been changed?

A. Three

7 What is the Preds' logo?

A. Saber-toothed tiger

8 Which Predators' goalie recorded the most shutouts in a single season?

A. Pekka Rinne

9 Which Predator is ranked number one in franchise history for most games played?

A. David Legwand

Key Words

All-Star: a game made for the best-ranked players in the NHL that happens mid-season. A player can be named an All-Star and then be sent to play in this game.

assists: a statistic that is attributed to up to two players of the scoring team who shoot, pass, or deflect the puck toward the scoring teammate

Calder Memorial Trophy: an award given out annually to the hockey player who is considered "the most proficient in his first year of competition" in the NHL

entry draft: an annual meeting where different teams in the NHL are allowed to pick new, young players who can join their teams

expansion: expansion in the NHL is marked by the addition of a new franchise. The league last expanded in 2000 when the Columbus Blue Jackets and Minnesota Wild joined the NHL.

franchise: a team that is a member of a professional sports league

logo: a symbol that stands for a team or organization

Norris Trophy: short for the James Norris Memorial Trophy, this trophy is awarded to the "defenseman who demonstrates throughout the season the greatest all-round ability in the position"

playoff: a series of games that occur after regular season play

rookie: a player age 26 or younger who has played no more than 25 games in a previous season, nor six or more games in two previous seasons

shutouts: games in which the losing team is blocked from making any goals

Index

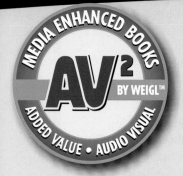

Log on to www.av2books.com

AV² by Weigl brings you media enhanced books that support active learning. Go to www.av2books.com, and enter the special code found on page 2 of this book. You will gain access to enriched and enhanced content that supplements and complements this book. Content includes video, audio, weblinks, quizzes, a slide show, and activities.

AV² Online Navigation

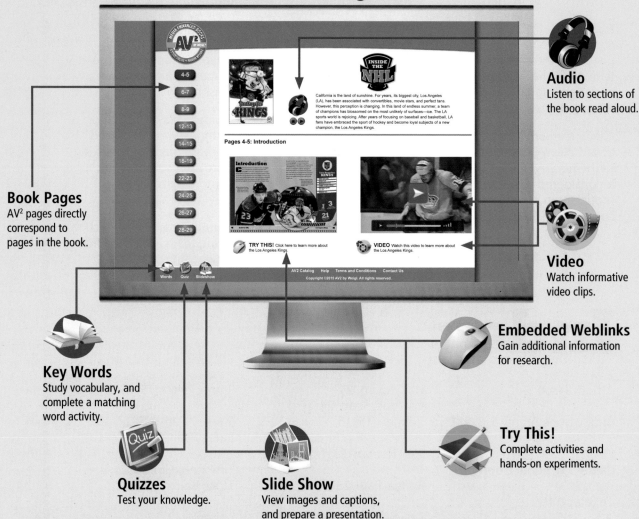

Audio
Listen to sections of the book read aloud.

Book Pages
AV² pages directly correspond to pages in the book.

Video
Watch informative video clips.

Embedded Weblinks
Gain additional information for research.

Key Words
Study vocabulary, and complete a matching word activity.

Try This!
Complete activities and hands-on experiments.

Quizzes
Test your knowledge.

Slide Show
View images and captions, and prepare a presentation.

AV² was built to bridge the gap between print and digital. We encourage you to tell us what you like and what you want to see in the future.

Sign up to be an AV² Ambassador at www.av2books.com/ambassador.

Due to the dynamic nature of the Internet, some of the URLs and activities provided as part of AV² by Weigl may have changed or ceased to exist. AV² by Weigl accepts no responsibility for any such changes. All media enhanced books are regularly monitored to update addresses and sites in a timely manner. Contact AV² by Weigl at 1-866-649-3445 or av2books@weigl.com with any questions, comments, or feedback.